Barack Obama's 2014
FOREIGN POLICY
OF THE U.S. GOVERNMENT

PAUL KREWENEK
OFFICE OF SHITS AND GIGGLES
WHITEHOUSE.GOV

ISBN: 1499306601

EAN-13:   978-1499306606

President Barack Obama

President Barack Obama

President Barack Obama

United States Foreign Policy

President Barack Obama

President Barack Obama

President Barack Obama

President Barack Obama

President Barack Obama

President Barack Obama

President Barack Obama

President Barack Obama

President Barack Obama

President Barack Obama

President Barack Obama

Made in the USA
Charleston, SC
07 May 2015